PLAYING
FROM ROUGH
GOLF AND THE NHS

GWEN

Illustrated by Patrick

authorHOUSE®

AuthorHouse™ UK Ltd.
1663 Liberty Drive
Bloomington, IN 47403 USA
www.authorhouse.co.uk
Phone: 0800.197.4150

Published by AuthorHouse   03/20/2014

ISBN: 978-1-4918-9666-2 (sc)
ISBN: 978-1-4918-9667-9 (e)

People are wonderful and unbelievably kind and generous in hard times so—

> *to a wonderful National Health Service which was there when I had need*
>
> *much gratitude to all the doctors, nurses and other staff who helped me whether in hospitals or the local surgery*
>
> *thanks for the practical help and wonderful support from friends and the care at the Mantzos Mansion.*

The Itchy Ear

Chapter 1

Beginning

I've been ripped off. Nothing unusual about that, money matters are not my province. I don't like shopping and shopping around for a good deal is a waste of fresh air as far as I am concerned. However, my ears still itch. I paid the chemist £5.45 for this ear spray having already tried Savlon and cotton wool buds and all of these have had no effect whatsoever. If anything the itch has got worse and is now in both ears having previously had single occupancy of the right ear. I determine to stop poking my fingers in my ear but this only lasts for a few hours as itch overrides determination.

I think the itch will reach my eardrum and I will go deaf. How will I cope in a deaf world? I suppose I will be able to get sub-titles on the television but will I hear the shout of 'fore' on the golf course as a missile heads towards my head at death causing speed? Will the Health and Safety Executive ban me from the game? I have only once been hit by a golf ball and that was on the back of my shoulder when I was playing in Turkey with a group of friends from Kent. I was standing in woods on the opposite side of the fairway to Pam, the perpetrator of the shot, and she gave no shout of 'fore'. I would have thought being a considerable distance from the fairway that I was safe. Pam, however, is a hopeless golfer and I should have known better. Nurse Timmins, our accompanying alleged first aider, poked the emerging bruise and declared me alive and so perpetrator Pam received by far the larger share of sympathy being traumatised by her failure to put the ball on the green. Life is just not fair.

I come to a tremendous decision. The weather is a little dull and I have no imminent golf match in the next few days so I will go and annoy the doctor with my itchy ear. An appointment with the trusty GP surgery is consequently made.

I am to see Dr Marvel who must be bored stiff by idiotic patients wasting her time with itchy ears, sore fingers, runny noses and the like.

"I've got an itchy ear"

Nevertheless, her professionalism takes over and she sticks one of her gadgets in my ears and declares I have 'Otitis Externa'.

I suspected as much having already looked up my symptoms on the internet. She sighs about people using cotton wool buds in their ears, fails to appreciate my dry humour when I ask if I should use something with a sharp point instead and gives me a withering look.

Dr Marvel tells me she is going to write a prescription for some eardrops and these will clear up the problem within a week. "Come back if it does not" says she; a statement she repeats as the look on my face must have displayed that 'coming back' was not going to be any kind of option for me.

A silence ensues while Dr Marvel looks up and writes the prescription.

This is a big mistake on her part as it gives me the opportunity for a good moan about my aching chest muscles to break the silence. I get this pain whenever I exert myself on the golf course. I have already put this down to the biceps tendonitis I developed last year as a result of spending too much time on both the golf course and practise ground. The climb from the seventh green to the eighth tee at Long Ashton Golf Club is the main place this pain strikes. I do not think Dr Marvel has the slightest interest in my golfing exploits so decide not to relate a stroke by stroke account of my last round.

I am wrong. Dr Marvel is more than interested now and whips out her stethoscope to listen to my chest; breathe in, breathe out she commands. She takes my blood pressure. Dr Marvel says "I want you to have an ECG and a blood test".

She must be mad!

What on earth for? What did she hear?

I am thinking the strain has got too much for this poor woman and I gawp at her. "I don't want to alarm you, it is just a precaution" says Dr Marvel. Well I am already alarmed.

I think about telling her that she has already diagnosed Otitis Externa and that she must now be confused as I am the same patient and the next one has not yet come through the door. I decide that she is confused and that my best course of action is to leave quietly and just do as instructed in order not to provoke her.

Chapter 2

The ECG

I attend the surgery two days later wondering what on earth I am doing here and make a bit of fuss about the loss of an 'armful of blood'. I have the blood says the nurse but I proclaim I felt nothing. Nurse looks pleased with herself.

Nurse now proceeds to stick pads over my body and to switch on her machine. She tells me to keep still and shut up, the latter of which she has probably been dying to say since I walked in the door. Nurse says the printout looks normal but that she was not properly qualified to interpret it and that I should see the doctor for feedback.

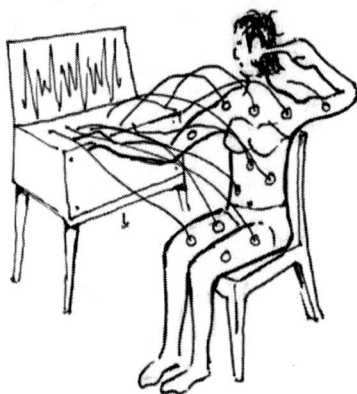

"But I've only got an itchy ear"

Two days later I see the doctor—not Doctor Marvel who they tell me has left. I think that this is very diplomatic of the receptionist as Dr Marvel obviously made a serious mistake over the ECG.

I, therefore, see Dr Graham. I think she said My ECG was normal as I knew it would be as are my kidneys, liver, blood sugar etc. I am waiting for the news about my cholesterol levels as I know this will not be good. Dr Graham shows a little surprise at the triglyceride level and asks if I fasted. What is she talking about? No one told me to fast so why on earth would I? The only thing I have fasted on is cream cakes. She declares the results invalid and tells me to arrange another blood test. How much blood do these people want?

Dr Graham says that she now wants me to have an ECG on a treadmill at the BRI. I am now wondering if any of the doctors in this surgery are OK.

Two days later I turn up at the BRI and am amazed by the presentation, cleanliness and prompt attention of the receptionist, not to mention the lack of a long waiting time. Honestly, what is the Daily Mail on about with its scary headlines?

The very pleasant nurse gets me ready taking more blood, my blood pressure and heart rate and proceeds to stick the little pads all over my body with a billion wires trailing from them.

Very interesting I think. Nurse explains what she needs to get my heart rate up to with a series of calculations and it comes to about 140 beats per minute. This woman is not on this planet as even when I go to the gym 125 beats per minute is about as much as I am going to strain myself towards.

Now we sit and wait till in comes The Hospital Doctor who introduces herself and off we go. I am plodding happily along on the treadmill when they decide to raise it to a gradient similar to the slopes of Kilimanjaro.

Hospital Doctor tells me to run faster by taking longer strides and I have doubts about her powers of observation. She has not noticed the short length of my legs. They only go as far as my hips while other people seem to have legs that go up to their armpits.

"What do you mean faster?"

I am now gasping for breath and have a little moan so everything is brought to a close. Hospital Doctor says it is marginal. Heaven knows what that means; either my heart is beating or it is not. Anyway she says she is just off to discuss the results with her consultant colleague. No doubt to have a cup of coffee.

On her return she declares that an angiogram would be the best option so they can see better what is going on and would I consider that. Would I consider it? Who is the doctor here? How on earth am I supposed to know?

Anyway my fate is decided—no harm done and I am now of the opinion that the entire staff of the NHS is gaga. Hospital Doctor gives me a letter for my GP which I duly deliver.

Dr Graham is still at the surgery much to my surprise and she gives me a prescription for medication to take while I wait for the angiogram. She says my blood pressure seems to be all over the place. I think their machines are all over the place. Protestations about I only came about an itchy ear are ignored. I tell Dr Graham that I considered myself immortal but she quickly disabuses me of this. I said I came in fit and well and the problem with doctors is that they make you ill. She quickly disabuses me of this as well as she said I was patently not ill. Well that's what she thinks!

Dr Graham gives me very explicit instructions on the use of the sub-lingual spray which she has now issued me with and tells me that I must stop when I have the pain and, if it does not go away with the spray, that I must dial 999 and call an ambulance.

She repeats all of this and I cannot believe what I am hearing. "Stop and dial 999 if the pain does not go away" she repeats. I just nod. **999**

Dr Graham has yet to learn that 999 is for stolen snowmen, headaches, lost cats and dogs and taxis that do not turn up on time. Why would I need an ambulance?

Ladies at the golf club are now interested in this on-going itchy ear saga and how I even got as far as the door of the BRI as the traffic and parking there are a nightmare. Learning that I went on my pedal bike, they are simply bemused.

The following letter arrives in a couple of days, which I can hardly believe given Daily Mail horror stories about the NHS.

> *Please ring the Cardiology Waiting List Office on the telephone number at the top of this letter **within the next 2 weeks between 9.00am and 4.00pm,** Monday to Friday to arrange a mutually convenient date for your procedure.*
>
> *If we do not hear from you within 2 weeks of the receipt of this letter, **we will assume that you no longer require this procedure. We will inform your GP and remove your name from the waiting list.***

The angiogram is arranged for the next week. There is a letter to my GP saying I am about to be admitted to hospital—are they joking? Admitted? I only agreed to pop in for an hour but apparently I am now to be admitted to hospital.

This is becoming more and more ridiculous. Reading the letter I spot the prospect of them informing my GP if I don't bother to turn up for the appointment. Thoughts of playing golf instead of turning up vacate my mind. Things worsen when I find I have to go for a preadmission assessment.

I have a lovely nurse called Dennis. He takes more blood, my blood pressure and another ECG even though I tell them I have just had one. Dennis asks me a million questions and then has to grope all of my body to check everything is there. He takes the pulse in every bit of my body and tells me he needs to take the pulse in my groin but unfortunately he is not very good at this as he cannot get his hand past the waist band of my trousers and is hopeless at undoing the button on my trousers.

He tells me I cannot drive after the angiogram and must stay with someone overnight. I ask him if I will be fit to play golf the next day and I receive another of those despairing looks which I am getting quite used to from the medical profession. He tells me I must not lift anything the next day and it will be a week till I use my arm for any kind of exertion.

Oh dear, this is becoming tiresome as it involves me making quite a change to my schedule for the next week. Burnham and Berrow Open is out as is the Bristol and Clifton Open. The organisers will not be pleased. Never mind I think. It is not every day I get groped by a handsome young man so I leave the hospital not too unhappy with how things are going. It is a pity that a lot of people's time is being wasted as all these tests will soon show I am fine.

Chapter 3

The Angiogram

I am picked up by friend Sam with children George and Emma on the school run and dumped at the door of the Cardiac Unit.

I enter the cardiac unit along with a few others, some of whom have been before, and they start to relate their previous experiences in which I have no interest. I go for a walk.

On return a nurse shows me to a changing cubicle telling me what to wear—a backless front. It is not thrilling and is accompanied by knickers which have a little frill on them presumably so women's can be differentiated from men's. I emerge and am shown to my bed.

No Dear! You've got it on back to front

There is lots of space, water, a chair and table. It is all quite nice. Better than some hotels I have stayed in.

Along comes the nurse for the usual blood sample and blood pressure test and then comes the doctor who introduces himself as Dr Ali and gives me a bit of a grope to check everything is there. He gropes my wrists and says the pulse is good and he will go in through my wrist and not groin; this must be a good thing.

Dr Ali wants to start and is a little short with the nurses as they are a little bit behind his timetable for events. He instructs a nurse who to get ready next and says he is taking me with him. I traipse after him and enter the operating room (technically called a catheter room). There are little steps for me to get onto the bed.

Dr Ali asks how I am feeling and I say fine but apprehensive so he tells nurse to give me a mild sedative. Then, off we go, a bit of pain in my wrist from the local anaesthetic. Then Dr Ali gives the orders, get the bed up, turn it this way and then all these cameras zoom in all over the place. I am having a good ride. Dr Ali then turns his screen and shows me my heart happily beating away with lots of very nice blood vessels. Honestly, how many people have seen their heart beating and lived. This is very interesting. To my misinformed brain that is that and all is well.

Now says Dr Assistant in the background I am going to inject the dye and you may feel a hot flush and you may feel as though you have wet yourself but don't panic, you have not. Well what have they been doing all this time? I thought we had finished and I just had to get dressed and go home. In goes the dye and I feel good with a lovely warm glow sweeping down my body.

Off we go again—merry go round on the bed, cameras whirring and hey a nice jolly time. Now Dr Ali turns his screen and starts to show me more things on my heart picture—lovely, very interesting I think.

"You need heart surgery" says Dr Ali.

I might nearly have had a fit but am relatively calm having had a sedative. "This cannot be", I say, "I am off to Peru walking the Inca Trail and Machu Picchu". There is obviously no logic to this statement so put it down to shock.

Dr Assistant says "mmmm—high altitude, low oxygen—not eminently suitable." "Was that a no?" I ask, "I only had an itchy ear".

"I've only got an itchy ear"

The team then proceed to tell me how good they are and how they operated on some famous person who went up Everest afterwards. Well everyone and their grandmother have been up Everest these days and I have no intention of going up Everest so this information is entirely irrelevant. While they agree my GP is good they proclaim how much better they are. "The Inca Trail will still be there next year" proclaims Dr Assistant.

"Well yes, but what about my pal Penny who I am going with. We have spent ages planning this and she will be disappointed". "Next year" they proclaim in chorus "you will be amazed at how good you feel next year" and repeat that the Inca Trail will still be there.

They are crazy. I will not be feeling good after they have finished messing about with me. Anyway I was already feeling good and my golf has been really good just to prove I am fit and healthy.

I am not allowed to leave the hospital as Dr Ali needs to talk to me. I return to my hotel like bed and am given a very acceptable lunch, chicken and salad sandwich, banana and fruit drink. I am now feeling comfortable and am sure that Dr Ali will be along soon to apologise for getting it all wrong. He has mixed me up with someone else. Alas this does not happen and instead Dr Ali turns up with a book and pictures of the problem. I will see a surgeon within a couple of weeks.

I appear to be well and truly done for and think I must be in dreamland. All of this cannot possibly be true.

I am now allowed to leave the hospital but only with an escort and enough medication to fill a wheelbarrow.

We drive to Orchard House and my mood is sombre. We have only just left the hospital grounds when a telephone call tells us to return as there is a letter for my GP. I am to keep the letter tonight and return with it to the hospital if I start to bleed to death.

Next morning and all is well. I am alive and have not bled to death. Sam takes me home and the letter is delivered to the GP. A call from the surgery in the afternoon asks me to call to review my medication.

I see Dr Grenfell who asks me if I know what is going on. I am bemused by this method of communication. The hospital informs me and I tell my GP. I suppose I could tell her anything. Then I think this cannot be and she is carrying out a test of my pea brain to see if it still working and if I understand the situation.

After yesterday's bombshell, it is a miracle that any part of my body is still working apart from the rear end. I make the point again that I only went about an itchy ear and how could I possibly believe that all of this is happening. She shows some sympathy.

My life is in tatters.

Chapter 4

Into Hospital

I turn up at hospital for yet another preadmission assessment. Arrays of nurses take blood and millions of measurements. My allocated surgeon, Mr Hutter, checks my comprehension of the situation, "Do I understand what is happening?" I have now watched the surgery on the internet so I get it.

Mr Hutter is satisfied and ensures there is little chance of my opting out of anything by firstly telling me he agreed with Dr Ali. Well these doctors have to stick together. He then gives an assessment of my chances of surviving a likely heart attack.

The chances seem to be about nil.

Another letter arrives—

I am writing to confirm that your name has been placed in the above Consultant's waiting list. You should be aware that in certain circumstances it may be necessary to offer you surgery with a different Consultant. You will, however, be advised of this prior to your admission.

Unless an approximate waiting time was discussed with you at your clinic appointment, *the waiting time for cardiac surgery is approximately* **2 months.**

When your name comes to the top of the waiting list we will contact you to discuss a mutually convenient date for your admission. **If you are available at short notice I would be grateful if you could contact me on the above telephone number.**

I receive the above letter giving a waiting time of around two months and explaining choice of dates.

I can go at short notice so make contact.

Life now continues in my new dreamland world and I am in a dilemma; how likely is this heart attack? Should I continue to play golf and exercise or descend to couch potato status? The last league match of the season is next week so to play or not to play? Golf captain decides this for me as she chickens out and says she is unwilling to have her year spoilt by my dropping dead on her watch. Scheduled golf in Spain is 'off' as travel insurance is now not available.

My dilemma is quickly resolved when I return home after a pleasant Tuesday morning on the golf course to a message on my answer machine asking me to telephone the hospital. I do and they say, "Are you able to come in tomorrow for surgery on Thursday?" I am a little stunned but agree to do so.

I have a bit of work to do cancelling and making new appointments. Wednesday arrives and I have a GP appointment in the morning. Dr Hardiman says I seem to have been having some fun as she astutely notices that things are not going too well for me at the moment. Something of an understatement I think as I have just about had it with everything. Dr Hardiman may think of it as fun but I am definitely not a happy bunny.

Well first the bad news and then Dr Hardiman gives me the good news that my cholesterol level is down to 5. This is of no interest to me at the moment as I am preoccupied with more immediate matters. In any case I am now so terrified that I have only been eating cardboard but refrain from imparting this information to Dr Hardiman as she is well pleased about my cholesterol level.

Sam now arrives to deliver me to the hospital. I wonder if Mr Hutter will be disappointed not to see me as I am now assigned to Professor Angelini. On arrival at the ward administration is not as quite as smooth as I had become used to but my name is found.

Alas, there is no bed available, then there is, then there is not. Sam points out that my name is on the board on the wall against a bed number and suggests I just go and hop into it. I restrain myself and Sam clears off.

My afternoon is spent having lots of checks. I meet my anaesthetist. We chat about golf and bridge. She loves bridge but two of her bridge four also play golf and discuss it incessantly. She dislikes this and has threatened death to her partner, who does not play golf, if she starts playing golf. She politely declares that her eyes might glaze over if I continue with a hole by hole account of my latest round of golf.

Tests all complete but the bed saga continues; there is a bed for me, there is not a bed for me and then there is a bed for me. By the time Sam returns it is clear there is not a bed. I am going home for the night only to return in the morning.

I depart the hospital with a clear list of instructions about eating, or rather not eating, about getting showered with the red goo they give me and not to mention what to stick up my nose. I have a time for arrival the following morning.

I am collected by Sam with the children the next morning and am now staying. The children are deposited at school.

I solve the bed problem by taking my own

There is now definitely a bed for me and Sam is now staying with me. She informs the nurse that this is to ensure I do not do a runner.

I am given the premedication and told not to get out of bed. They stick a thing on my bed saying 'nil by mouth'. I keep telling Sam that this premed is having no effect whatsoever. She tells me later that I spent the next hour giggling.

Off to the operating room and all I remember is that they cannot get the damned anaesthetic needle into my wrist. Someone swears about this. After a couple of tries, they must have managed it as I know nothing more.

Chapter 5

Post Surgery

I assume that my bypass surgery took place but I know nothing about it. I assume my heart is now all repaired and bandaged up nicely. I hope they have put the elastoplast in the right place as I do not want blood dripping into my body cavity. Sam tells me I woke in intensive care to proclaim "I'm alive—where is the champagne?" I have no knowledge of this and am somewhat suspicious about its occurrence.

I have little knowledge about anything much over the next few days. I remember a nurse giving me a wash in bed—I guess this is a bed bath. I remember being asked if I knew that I had pressed the morphine button 14 times in the last hour. I have no knowledge of this either. I do not remember seeing any morphine button.

Eventually, after a couple of days, I managed a shower and a physiotherapist turned up to take me for a walk. I didn't like to tell him that I had already done the walk on which he accompanied me. A few visitors start to turn up and bring some welcome fruit and I cannot remember eating much food apart from this.

Friend Pauline turns up and is disappointed to find me out of bed when she had expected to see me lying in bed with thousands of tubes sticking out. I restrain myself from showing her the various tubes and wires sticking out of my body.

A porter with a wheelchair arrives at the same time as Pauline which I assume is to take me to the cardiac ward away from high dependency but actually to take me for an X-Ray.

◄ **X-Ray**

Anyone want a ride?

Anyway, I decide I am perfectly able to walk and am not going in the wheelchair.

I suddenly feel nauseous and think I am going to vomit. A nurse produces what Pauline called a vomit hat. I start a prolonged coughing fit which no amount of pressure from the towel on my chest brings any relief. I am unable to speak to Pauline or even acknowledge her presence. I am carted off to X-Ray coughing violently and needless to say in the wheelchair. There is not much choice about this as I am taken coughing so violently that I am unable to walk. Perhaps I am not as well as I thought.

On return from X-Ray Pauline has vanished and the coughing has ceased. I am back in my bed in high dependency as there would seem to be no bed in the cardiac ward.

Chapter 6

The Cardiac Ward

The following day they have found a bed in the cardiac ward for me and I am transferred in a wheel chair. I now share a ward with 3 other inmates. They are a lot worse off than I am and as I get to know things about them, I begin to realise that our public hospitals are by and large full of a lot of sadness.

My anaesthetist turns up together with a pal of hers and they have a chat about my dressing gown, which I inform them was bought in Vietnam for about £10. I tell them I have been suffering with coughing and will never ever go near a GP or hospital again.

Anaesthetist's pal says it is just like child birth. She only had one child as she was not going to suffer the birth process again. Anaesthetist tells me not to worry and I will soon be up and running round the golf course again and getting my handicap lower. She is having a laugh as the way I am feeling I doubt I will ever walk round a golf course again never mind hit a ball.

Mid-morning of my second day in the cardiac ward is greeted with instructions about getting into bed during the day. I do not consider this to be any kind of problem as the other three inmates spend their entire day or at least ninety percent of it in bed. However, nurse in charge tells me to just let her know if I want to get into bed and she will give me a blanket so that I do not disturb the freshly made bed. This would obviously give them bad marks as it made it look as though they had not done anything that morning and it made the place untidy.

I am fed up and given everything that has happened I really do not care whether or not the place is tidy. I remind myself that only dull women have tidy houses.

That night I manage to get some sleep despite the ramblings of fellow inmate number 1 who thinks she will go swimming the next day and seems to be unaware whether she is in bed or not. Whatever condition she is in, she wants the opposite—if in bed she needs to be out of bed and if out of bed she needs to be in bed. This constant movement is brought to a halt when the nurse puts the rails of the bed up.

I drop off to sleep and am woken around 5am by the very quiet calls for a nurse from fellow inmate number 2 in the adjacent bed. These are so quiet as to be unlikely to attract any attention whatsoever. The cries continue to drive me to distraction so I suggest to her that she pushes her button if she needs some help. This is an act of greater magnitude than she can possibly manage as she cannot find the button.

This is quite worrying for me as this woman has had a huge collection of doctors and nurses around her bed for a good deal of time the previous day. I ask her if she would like me to push my button for her and she assents. Unfortunately, I now have to find my button and this involves movement so I am yet again not a happy bunny.

Along comes the nurse and I explain it is for the adjacent inmate who she swiftly attends to. This sad inmate needs to know where she is, as she thought her daughter took her home last night and obviously she is not actually at home. The nurse is very patient and explains that she is safe and being looked after in hospital.

It is now 8am and a bright and breezy nurse comes along and declares, "I need two of you to get out of bed now so I can change the sheets and, when I have done that, I am going to tip the other two of you out".

I quickly realise that as far as the other three inmates are concerned that she might as well save her breath as they are now well and truly fast asleep having between them been engaged in some kind of activity most of the night. I drag myself out of bed and lock myself in the bathroom where I can wash and dress in relative peace.

My consultant cardiologist says I can leave hospital today providing my blood test proves to be OK. I say he is mine as obviously he has nothing else to do. The hospital has had so much of my blood that I wonder if they have to feed blood sucking bats. A wait of several hours takes place till all is announced to be well.

A few more things need to be done not least of which is obtaining yet another wheelbarrow full of pills from the hospital pharmacy.

There is also a letter for my GP. She must be sick of reading them.

Chapter 7

Release from Hospital

I am free to go Sam, George and Emma arrive to escort me to the Mantzos Mansion. I see the open air and it is very strange. I have become institutionalised in hospital for 6 days and now have to survive in an ordinary world with ordinary people going about their ordinary business.

How very strange!

The first morning of my release I manage to get up, washed and dressed although this takes a long time and a lot of effort. I spend the day on the sofa in the sitting room in a position where I will eventually be known as 'the blob'.

Around 11.00am things start to go wrong and I embark on a series of coughing fits which are agony. By 4pm I am exhausted and realise things are not right. A series of telephone calls follows with the buck eventually being passed to the GP and an appointment made.

Chapter 8

Dr Dilly

Dr Dilly has a lovely name even if she does not look old enough to be a doctor. I tell her I have been coughing on and off for most of the day, that the pain is bad and I am anxious. "You look sweaty and exhausted" she states "do you mind if I examine you?"

Dr Dilly has a good listen to my chest with her stethoscope and is not happy with what she hears. She says my left lung has not fully inflated after the surgery and she thinks I have a chest infection and need to be readmitted to hospital.

I explain that I have just escaped and that another escape will prove difficult. Dr Dilly does not realise that the locks on the hospital doors are not to keep intruders out but to keep patients in. I tell her there will not be a bed—any excuse will do at this stage. Alas Dr Dilly is brighter than this and I am not going to be allowed to use this one. Dr Dilly assures me that finding a bed is her prerogative and not for me to be worrying about.

A period of protracted negotiation follows as the hospital has dumped me out with only some paracetemol ground is conceded. Hence, Dr Dilly prescribes some pain killers and antibiotics with an agreement that I will go to the hospital later that night or the following morning if I have not improved.

She is emphatic that it must be an improvement and I will need to see her again on Monday morning.

All the chemists are by this time closed so a trip to Sainsbury is needed to collect the medication.

We arrive home without further incident and about 30 minutes after taking the medication, I am feeling a lot better. I manage some food with the rest of the family and then Sam packs me off to bed with the rest of the children.

I don't sleep a lot but am warm and comfortable and the next morning I am able to rise feeling a lot better. Paramedics George and Emma arrive to check I am still alive. Saturday and Sunday pass without incident and I have even been walking outside—somewhat gingerly but there is progress.

Sunday night sees my pillow arrangement collapsing and me unable to move much so, when I hear Sam arising at her usual unearthly hour in the middle of the night (5.00am), I call for assistance and tell her I am stuck. This is met with considerable mirth by her but after her giggling fit passes she does help me to sit up.

Dr Dilly emerged very promptly when I signalled my arrival at the surgery on Monday and relief passed over her face as she astutely spots that I am still alive (I think it was the movement that gave her a clue) and looking better. The poor woman had obviously been a little worried that she had not insisted on my return to hospital. However, I congratulate her on the right decision and then mutual congratulations follow and my escape from hospital is now complete.

Chapter 9

Convalescence

We return to the Mantzos convalescent home where I continue to blob on the settee. Jill Lambert turns up to comfort me and we enjoy watching the end of the Ryder Cup together upon the end of which I blob out again.

I have now managed to walk to the bottom of the drive and back and even offered to go horse riding with Paramedics George and Emma but was informed that as I could not do that before I was certainly not going to do it now.

Paramedic Emma is now well trained in the removal of dressings which unbelievably she does not flinch at. Mother informs me it would be a different matter if they were on her. She is also by now an experienced surgical stocking fitter.

Paramedic George performs the operation to remove the hospital identification badge on my wrist as it is now deemed that I am sufficiently sane to be able to identify myself without its help.

Chapter 10

Returning Home

Another Monday arrives and it is now time for the blob to leave the care of the Mantzos Family and return to her own abode under the care of friend Penny. This all goes well and so arrangements are made for Penny to play golf with the ladies on Tuesday. The blob is becoming quite animated so she walks the course with Penny. Lunch in the clubhouse follows.

Everyone is surprised to see me out and looking OK. Arrangements are made for a repeat on Thursday. However, Wednesday follows Tuesday and does not go that well following the exertions of Tuesday. I spend most of the day asleep or in a similar comatose sort of state unable to do anything.

On Thursday Penny declares that a slower start to the day and a shorter stroll round the golf course are required in order to avoid a repeat of Wednesday.

The next day there are issues with the wound on my chest. It is emitting evil looking gooey stuff and the medical team of Sam, Emma, Penny and I decide that something is not right. This results in yet another trip to the local surgery and I see the nurse. She looks at the unpleasant mess and decides a dressing is needed. Then she looks again and calls Locum Doctor Number 1. Oh dear, more antibiotics are prescribed.

Nausea now sets in, it passes and then returns. On reporting this to Nurse Sandra during a scheduled visit to change dressings, she refers me to Locum Doctor Number 2. She declares I am probably intolerant to the prescribed antibiotic and prescribes a different one. Further visits to Nurse Sandra ensue as she checks wound healing. The sensitive skin on my chest declares it has had enough of dressings by becoming red and developing a few new wounds which gush blood.

Nurse Sandra checks this out but is unimpressed by my description of gushing blood and satisfies herself that this means a few drops. However, healing has taken place and assignations with Nurse Sandra are coming to an end.

A further visit to Dr Dilly and my weight is back to normal so I can stop taking the water extracting pills. Great is my joy as I will be able to reduce my visits to the toilet considerably. Staying in bed all night will be a welcome outcome.

Chapter 11

Communications

Alas I have disrupted the system by having surgery earlier than planned and swapping surgeons. I receive a variety of letters offering both postoperative and preoperative checks. A few telephone calls result which cause some consternation and confusion over what surgery I have had. I inform one receptionist, perhaps rather abruptly, that I would prefer not to have a further bypass.

I receive a letter about the rehabilitation programme and turn up for a first interview and assessment. On arrival at outpatients my name is not on the receptionist's list. She is unable to cope with this and her subsequent frustration is manifest. The waiting room is crowded, I am not feeling great and she is getting on the one nerve I have left.

The sister in charge sorts it out. The nurse from the rehabilitation team checks how I am doing and says I can start the programme and that it is OK for me to have sex now. It is just wonderful what you can get on the NHS these days.

Friends do not know whether I am in or out of hospital and the hospital is often uncertain. A few visitors turn up to see me only to find that I have been kicked out.

This results in my receiving the following letter and invoice.

Hitchcock & Holt Social Services to The Queen

On Saturday our specialised team of social workers called on you to determine what, if any, help you may require on your return home.

You may appreciate that lugging bedpans, walking frames and Stena lifting equipment through the hospital was no mean task. We found that 6 days of you was enough and they had thrown you out.

Regretfully we must take this affair seriously as the two social workers had to take a week off to recuperate. With this in mind I enclose an invoice for the aborted visit. Should you find it difficult to pay the said invoice I am sure the social will assist; in any event we would appreciate payment by return.

PS We wish you a speedy recovery

Invoice

Aborted Visit to Hospital	*(Fuel & Time)*	*£2.99*
Recovery Time	*(Week in Cornwall)*	*TBA*
2 bunches of black grapes	*(2 for 1 Sainsbury's)*	*£3.00*

Tuesday Lunch at the Golf Club is becoming an interesting debate about medical issues. I am able to contribute with my now vast knowledge of all matters to do with the heart and can offer guided tours of the BRI. There is a great deal of expertise at the table on all manner of medical issues including the many golfing injuries we have endured between us.

We decide to run a consultancy service and determine that we will be called 'The Loose Women Medical Consultancy Service'. We will advertise and let local surgeries know so they can make referrals. We will not charge for this service but people attending will have to pay for their own lunch.

Chapter 12

Rehabilitation

Penny and I have become sad over our cancelled holiday so a couple of lunches at Raymond Blanc's restaurant in Cabot Circus are required. Further recuperation is, however needed. As we had to dump the holiday in Peru we decide a cruise in the Caribbean in February will be eminently suitable as we need sun and I am feeling very sad.

This is booked and things are looking up.

The holiday is booked but my worldwide travel insurance has increased from £0 to £140. My bank has dumped anything worthwhile that they offer by putting 'excluded' against anything medical on my insurance policy. This effectively means they are not insuring me to travel. This is not very nice of them and makes me sadder still.

On our cruise Penny and I have booked lots of activities without realising that most of them carried warnings not to take part if you had a heart problem. I decided that any such heart problems had been fixed so ignored the warnings and off we went—a bit of zip wiring, horse riding (well mine was a mule that would not move), scuba and a little sail.

We were well happy!

On return home, I turn up for my first attendance at the rehabilitation programme. This starts with a talk from a dietician. It is all pretty obvious but in the audience are two or three people who are unable to keep quiet and see their role as being to demonstrate their expertise in the dietary field to all of us and to keep the dietician on the right track.

This is followed by an assessment and my pulse, weight and blood pressure are by now pretty good. This is not surprising given the size of my pharmacy. A physiotherapist now leads the exercise session and before the warm up is complete, one out of the group of eight is lying on the bed. He emerges later to join in again but is quickly replaced on the bed by another member of the group.

Exercise is followed by relaxation on a mattress with pillows. The room is darkened and a tape is played; one of those where your body slowly gets heavier starting with the eyes and moving downwards. I spend the time thinking about what I need to buy from Marks and Spencer and on completion of the mental shopping list need the tape to hurry up and reach the heavy toes bit.

Session 3 of rehabilitation sees a change to the usual pattern. The speaker this week is not going to allow me to sit and relax. Participation is required. We are split into groups and outcome the large poster sheets which we have to fill with our knowledge and comments. I try to be helpful by suggesting that one of the benefits of exercise is that you can eat more.

I am now starting to feel well enough to have a go at golf and so emerge onto the putting green before my regular lunch with the ladies. All goes well and I find I am now also eating well.

Alas snow and cold weather follow so my return to the main golf course is delayed. Just as well because my attempts at hitting a ball in the range were completely unsuccessful and I had to give up. Oh well, not to worry. Spring will be here soon and I will be off on the course with the bluebells.

I do eventually return to golf a little too soon and start playing in competitions and matches. I realise this when towards the end of one tournament I am at the point of collapse. I am exhausted, have a pain in the chest and am vomiting. I am terrified. I resolve to take things more easily.

Back to golf

I am now well on the road to full recovery but—
I still have an itchy ear!

Chapter 13

Good Times Return

Well I have reshaped my swing, been to the gym and don't eat cream cakes any more. My golf is good and I am onto winning ways again.

I need to get fit

Travel Insurance is costing me a small fortune but holidays have also returned. I have one minor problem in that my ears are blocked and I am about to fly to Jordan for Petra and the Dead Sea. I think the doctor can scrape the wax out of my ear and so pay a visit to the surgery.

Dr Gibbs is new but has the same gadgets as Dr Marvel so she has a look in my ear and declares there is no wax blocking them but she spots the problem. There are apparently lots of little bubbles in my middle ear and not to worry it will pass. So that is that. I am packing to go away and sleeping is a bit of a problem as something in the house is humming at night and I cannot find which machine is making the noise. I hope the house will not blow up while I am away.

However, off I go and the noise goes with me and furthermore it comes back home with me. After a month at home with this racket I am finding life increasingly difficult. Research indicates I have tinnitus and it is driving me round the twist.

I see Dr Gibbs again and tell her aliens have got into my ears and are making a constant row. She is not impressed but decides that, as my ears have now been a pain for months that she will make a referral to Ear Nose and Throat. A hospital appointment is made but I am not full of hope as a little more research indicates that there are no miracle cures for tinnitus. There don't seem to be any cures at all, never mind miracle ones. Well hope springs eternal so I attend the appointment.

A very nice hospital doctor tells me I have some hearing loss at the higher frequencies. She suggests that I have some therapy and that she will also arrange a scan of my head to check there are no problems with the auditory nerve. She is 95% certain there is not and if there is will deal with it then.

I turn up for therapy. This is counselling by any other name but I begin to get the message that there are things I can do to help myself. Relaxation seems important so perhaps I should stop running round like a twenty year old blue arsed fly.

A few helpful suggestions are made. Watching a candle flame might not be the best idea as after a few drinks I will probably burn the house down. I buy a wave machine as I am sure this will help me get to sleep.

I buy a model that sprays aromas as well as giving a choice of sounds. I go to bed that night full of excitement at the prospect of using my new toy. I mess around for some time choosing the aromas I will use and then a bit longer trying to insert it into the contraption. I give in and go hunting for the instructions. These have been thrown in the bin so there is now a mess on the kitchen floor. Find them and then success!

Alas my new toy is not all that effective but things are a little better and my expectations were perhaps a little high. Unfortunately a fan blows the aroma into the room and it drowns out the relaxing sound. I switch off the fan. It takes an eternity to find the right switch and I find I have also turned off the relaxing sound. Exhausted by all of this I fall asleep.

Things are not getting better!

My bedroom is so full of gadgets that it really is not surprising that I cannot get off to sleep easily. Red lights are just all over the place.

Well the letter eventually arrives giving a time for my scan. Two days later another letter arrives cancelling this one and giving me another time. Lots of apologies from them so no problem. On arrival for the scan I get another of those amazing hospital backless fronts and am slotted into the contraption. I have not had a scan before and am not sure what to expect.

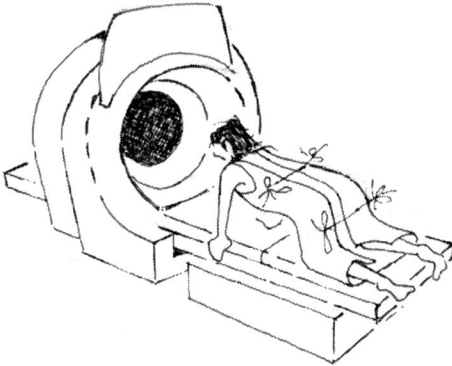

"I'm not going in there on my own"

There is a lot of banging and other noises and then I am pulled out and the nurse comes back into the room all smiles and niceness. She tells me the radiographer is not happy with the clarity of the scan and wants to do it again after she has injected a dye. In goes the dye, in I go and the whole process is repeated.

Monday morning 9.00am immediately following the scan and a nurse from St Michael's is on the phone asking if I can attend at 11.15 tomorrow for feedback on my scan. I can and I think the NHS are getting better and better as this is very quick. I think they are seeing me quickly because they have spotted the problem and have the magic cure. Hooray!

Gwen

I turn up for my appointment and my name is not on the list. Oh dear because I have been here before. However, the ultra-efficient receptionist goes off to check and says everything is fine and I will be seen soon. Much better than the last time I had this problem. I am to see Mrs Douglas.

Chapter 14

Mrs Douglas

Mrs Douglas heads the staff list so must be the tops. This together with the expected miracle cure is all good news. A nurse calls me and says she will be sitting in. I know not why. Mrs Douglas is not the Hospital Doctor I saw previously. I sit down and say that with this speed I must be at death's door. Mrs Douglas does not contradict me—a trifle worrying.

Mrs Douglas says the scan showed no problems with the auditory nerve but displayed an unrelated problem about which I obviously had no knowledge and no symptoms. She tells me I have a meningioma—a brain tumour.

She is having a laugh.

I stare at Mrs Douglas. She says she has made a referral to David Porter, a neurosurgeon at Frenchay and told my GP.

She is not having a laugh.

I assume I have cancer and am going to die now. Mrs Douglas says the tumour is benign and I have not got cancer. Oh well I am not going to die—or not immediately anyway. Mrs Douglas tells me that the radiographer spotted it and was sufficiently concerned to telephone her.

Mrs Douglas asks if I have any questions but I am completely out of my head. She says I can go back any time if I think of something. The nurse offers me tea but I decline. Nevertheless she insists on walking me to the hospital door.

The good times did not last long

My Life is in Tatters Again

I am utterly unable to do anything. My mind is blank. I watch television but have no idea what was on. I cannot move.

I try to move and I go for lunch at the golf club. Joannie asks me what I have been up to that morning and why had I not turned up for golf? I tell my pals I have been to the hospital and they have told me I have a brain tumour. It all goes a bit quiet. Oh God, we have a golf match against Henbury tomorrow and I don't think I can remember how to play.

I don't sleep but the next morning I determine I just have to get up and get on with it. My mind is a fog but I turn up for the match. I play after a fashion, my legs are like jelly and unsurprisingly I lose. What is worse is that I don't care.

Realisations dawn upon me—The scan was done twice because the radiographer had spotted the meningioma and needed to inject the dye to make it show up more clearly. The hospital appointment following the scan was so quick because bad news was coming. The nurse was present to pick me up from the floor if I collapsed. I guess Mrs Douglas is fairly used to giving bad news to people.

Minor Ear Problem 1—outcome—*heart bypass*

Minor Ear Problem 2—outcome—*brain tumour*

I am going to the Long Ashton Surgery tomorrow to tell Dr Grenfell that, if I ever turn up there again with any kind of ear problem, I am simply to be told to clear off. The NHS cannot afford me any longer and I cannot take any more. While I am there Dr Grenfell can prescribe some sleeping pills.

Two days have passed and I am becoming calmer. The panic has subsided. The weekend comes and I actually sleep. By Monday new practicalities emerge. I am soon off to Portugal for a week of bridge and golf. Panic starts again and to make matters worse, those I am going with are also worried that I will not be going. Research on the internet along with no symptoms indicates there is no reason for me not to go. As far as I know the thing could have been there for years and some people think that this could explain a lot.

Travel insurance raises its ugly head. HSBC have already kicked me out following bypass procedures. However, I do have a year's worldwide insurance with another firm—at a cost! Well I did till they heard the latest and they then kicked me out. I rowed with them but I might as well have saved my breath. I did succeed in getting a refund from them. I am now trawling the internet for some insurance as my broker is useless. After hours of form filling and extortionate quotes, I eventually get insurance for the week in Portugal for a relatively modest £40.00. Immediate problems are over.

Off to Portugal

Chapter 15

David Porter

This is my consultant, a talented and experienced neurosurgeon, and I have an appointment with him at Frenchay. Everyone says how good they are at Frenchay and this guy looks good on paper. Of course I don't much care how good he is as I don't really feel like having my skull ripped open and my brain messed about with by anyone.

At reception the nurse asks me to use the machine on the wall to let the Doctor know I have arrived. She laughs and says she will see me again in a few minutes when I have found out how it doesn't work which is most of the time. You wave the bar code on your letter under the machine and in time it works.

The waiting room is pretty dismal and the people in it look pretty dismal. Some of them look pretty sick. We don't have to wait too long and David Porter emerges. He asks a few basic questions and shows me the scan of my brain.

I look and blurt out that it is huge, the tumour that is not my brain.

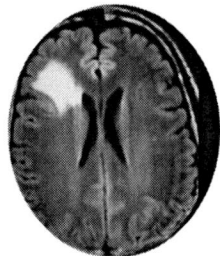

Doctor says it is not huge and is actually small and measures it on the screen with a pretty nifty device. He gives me some figures but I have no idea now what they were.

Mr Porter plays about with his screen showing me lots of different views and says—

it is small suggesting I should not have surgery

there is water in the brain around it showing it is growing suggesting I should have surgery

it lies in the plane of the optic nerves suggesting I should have surgery.

So as I see it 2 to 1 for surgery so that means none. He presents a pretty depressing account of life after surgery—driving (i.e. none), tiredness and not to mention the upset and tears. I check with David Porter things I will be able or not able to do or not do after the surgery.

Question 1—Will I be able to play golf? **Answer**—you people and your handicaps! You will know when.

Question 2—Will I be able to play Bridge? **Answer**—not as well as you do now.

Question 3—Will I be able to do the Times Crossword? **Answer**—can you do it now? **My Response**—well no and this ends this conversation.

I can choose surgery or monitoring. Well apparently waiting 6 months will make no difference to any surgery and I will be able to fit in another year of golf so that is that decided. The truth is I cannot face more surgery so will bury my head in the sand and hope everything goes away.

I just don't want to know

David Porter says he wants me to have some field of vision tests and arrangements are made for this. When I turn up the nurse tells me that only 3 of her 5 appointments have turned up that day and that is not unusual. What a waste!

Chapter 16

The Six Month Wait

This seemed a good idea at the time but did not turn out to be so great. Life did continue reasonably well but I spent a lot of time being driven nuts thinking about my future. Every minor ache or pain was put down to the brain tumour. Even short visits to Europe cost a small fortune for insurance and it took me ages to find acceptable ones on the internet. Most of them seem to be concerned about whether or not I could walk a hundred yards on the flat. If they knew the size of the hill I live on, they would not need to ask.

A letter comes from GP asking if I am depressed or getting no enjoyment from life and asking me to make an appointment with GP if this is so. Well, of course I am depressed. I am a lifelong supporter of Sunderland Football Club and even when they are good they depress you. You could not possibly get any enjoyment from watching them play. They are certainly not good at the moment and the threat of relegation looms.

To make matters worse they have sacked the manager and appointed an alleged fascist as the new manager. The local mining union have withdrawn support for the club. I don't think there were many members in this union anymore.

The local press is full of outrage. David Milliband has resigned as one of the directors in protest. Well he is off to the USA anyway. Perhaps Ed will take his place.

Despite all of this I am not making any visits to GP as they mostly end up with my life in tatters and needing major surgery.

Oh joy of joys Sunderland has beaten Newcastle; all is forgiven and the new manager is now a hero. I am ecstatic. Newcastle fans are not happy and there is a bit of trouble in Newcastle. One maniac Newcastle fan punches a police horse in its face.

When you grow up in a mining village near Sunderland, your only entertainments are school and the football club. The match result on Saturday determines the factory productivity and community mood the following week. Therefore you are hooked as a fan of Sunderland for life and you also have an aversion to Newcastle Football Club.

Further joy Sunderland have beaten Everton and the new manager is a saint. They may escape relegation with a decent result against Aston Villa. Alas we are back to old times as they barely bother to turn up at Aston Villa and get hammered. Relegation looms its head again. GP appointment coming up to deal with the resulting depression.

Appointment for my next scan comes up and off I go to Frenchay. I do all the registration stuff and go to a small waiting room where a couple are already in residence. It is 10.00am and my appointment is 10.15am. The resident couple tell me they are running late as they have a sick child 'in there'. They tell me their appointment was 9.45am.

I wonder if I now have time to go for a cup of coffee. Good job I didn't as the nurse emerges promptly at 10.15am and calls me in. I feel the outrage of the couple who were there before me and with an earlier appointment. The hairs on their necks were erect.

The scan goes well and the nurse injects what I now know is Gadolinium dye for the second bit. It gives contrast to the meningioma on scans.

Not again—I don't understand why they get impatient with me. I have the backless front on the right way round.

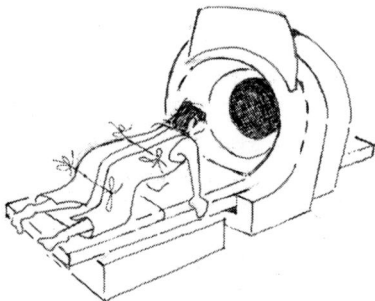

"Oh no, not this thing again"

Meanwhile Sunderland have managed a draw against Stoke but are still in dire trouble. Further plans for GP appointment to treat the depression.

Oh joy of joys again, Wigan lose and give Sunderland and half a dozen other clubs hope. GP appointment no longer necessary.

The last match of the season against Spurs will be a nail biter so perhaps I should prepare the ambulance service for a call regarding my heart attack now.

Back to the golf course and this is not going too well either.

The sight of a 3 inch putt almost gives me a nervous breakdown.

Sunderland are driving me to distraction after they have only drawn against Southampton. Wigan win the cup which is great for them. If they win their last two matches, Sunderland are down unless they draw against Spurs and then Aston Villa are down.

Things are tense but Wigan manage to lose against Arsenal *and are therefore relegated and Sunderland are safe. Hooray!

Roll on next season.

Chapter 17

More Problems

My knee is f . . . . d. It keeps collapsing and locking. I am fed up with all of this as I will have to go and see GP again. Dr Grenfell is bound to find something else wrong as well as the knee. You have to wait ages for an appointment with your own GP. In the meantime I fantasise about having the surgery to remove the brain tumour and to repair the knee together.

I thought Emma was fantasising about having some chickens and was sure her parents would never allow it. Emma now has some chickens. I decide that I will have some chickens and give it a lot of thought. They will be a calming influence on me. I need the garden to look good so invest in a state of the art lime green *Omlet Eggloo Coop*. It costs far too much so to save money I do not buy the run as I have lots of chicken wire to make one.

Sam and Emma arrive with chickens and food etc. They bring one grey and one ginger chicken. Both are placed in the enclosure and named Emma and George. I go to put them to bed that night and they panic at the sight of me. Emma jumps out of the enclosure and while I am trying to catch her George jumps out. All is at panic stations. I catch George and lock him in the coop. I go after Emma and spend about an hour trying to catch her. She flies everywhere and I thought hens could not fly. She flies over the fence to the bottom of the garden and I pursue her despite the darkness. She goes through the hedge into the neighbour's garden. They are away but I trespass and nearly break a leg looking for her. At least the people on the other side did not call the police.

Kentucky here we come

Emma has gone. Only George remains and he is sulking at the loss of Emma. Wednesday arrives and there is a hell of a noise from George. He is being attacked by a ginger cat that has broken into his enclosure. He escapes fleetingly but the cat is chasing George round the lawn so I rush out to chase the cat away. Alas George flies over the fence and the cat flies over the fence after him. There is a terrible noise from the garden below as the cat destroys George.

It has not been a good day

 my hen has been destroyed

 I have lost my golf match

 I have had a dispute with one of the green staff

 Murray has won at tennis and I don't like him.

I do not feel well!

I decide to raise my spirits by investing more funds in this venture and buy the proper *Omlet* enclosure together with some new chickens. The new enclosure took 2 hours to construct despite instructions informing me it would take 30 minutes.

I have calculated it will take about ten years of egg supply for me to break even and this does not include the cost of feeding them!

Oh joy of joys, word has got round Long Ashton regarding my missing hens and a neighbour phones to say she has them. George had successfully fought off the killer cat.

The hens are installed in their new super home.

Having watched a video on U-Tube showing you how to do it, I clip the wings of my chickens. They can no longer fly off.

They return home

I tell everyone that I have healing abilities as I have resurrected my hens. I hope Dr Grenfell has similar powers for my knee. Perhaps she can sort out the brain tumour too as I have not yet been notified of a further appointment with Mr Porter and it has been months since the scan. My records have probably been left on a bus.

A match at Knowle has left me aching especially my back. I go for some physiotherapy which costs me another small fortune. I still ache. I continue with lots of exercise. My knee stops collapsing and locking. It does not feel right but there has been a significant improvement and I determine to continue with the exercise in the hope of making a full recovery.

With this in mind I cancel my appointment with Dr Grenfell. She will just have to make do with someone else. This is a good thing as she will not be able to find anything else wrong with me if she does not see me. I wonder how long I can keep this up.

Oh joy of joys my chickens have started to lay eggs! There is, however, a downside to these chickens. I spent a small fortune on a lovely home for them but they don't care and sh . . . . all over it. Attempts at house training are hopeless.

Chapter 18

Problems at The Golf Course

I am playing golf with Pam and it is very hot. Pam is playing well and pars the eighth hole which is quite an achievement considering she put her drive in the hedge.

Awash with excitement she proceeds to put her drive from the ninth tee into a bunker. On arrival at the bunker she spots that the ball is not lying well. It is all too much for her so Pam now declares she is feeling unwell. She is grey.

Normally on the golf course there is someone behind you giving you hell and someone in front holding you up and a crowd of green keepers digging up bunkers. Well there was no one in reach with a mobile phone and I had to 'sprint' to the club house and 'sprint' back.

Attempts are made by various club members to get the heart machine to the ninth green. Alas they cannot open the box.

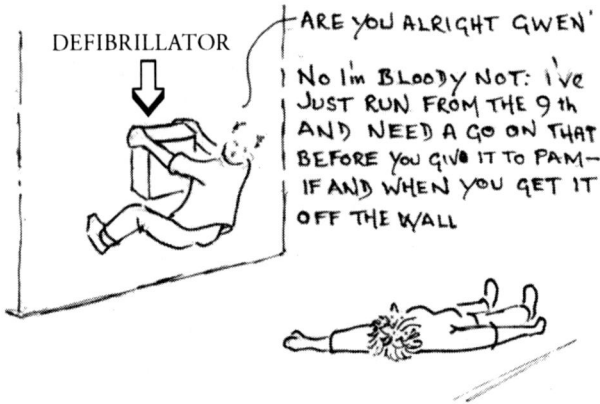

I now have to 'sprint' to the gate to direct the ambulance. It nearly knocks me over as I flag it down.

Good job she is not actually having a heart attack. She would be dead. All kinds of technology are attached to Pam and a second ambulance called to take her to hospital. It is 2.00pm and the green keepers finish work. They secure the gates ensuring one ambulance is safely locked in and the other one locked out.

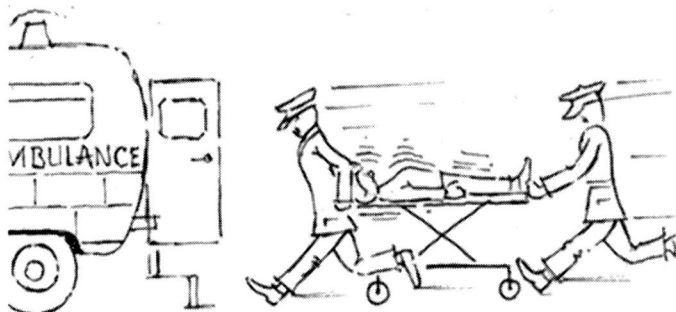

HURRY UP MATE
THEY LOCK THE
GATE AT 2 pm

IN THAT CASE WE
ARE LOCKED IN-
ITS 2.30 pm

Vice-Captain Charles sorts this out and flags down the next ambulance with blue light flashing. We now have 3 ambulances. Alas we have flagged down the wrong ambulance on its way to another emergency.

SORRY MATE - THIS
ONE IS TAKEN you'll
HAVE To FIND ANOTHER

In the end all is well, the ambulance people are magnificent and Pam is off to hospital. The hospital has ambulances pouring in. You cannot believe it. Heaven knows how they cope.

The doctor is fantastic and tells Pam he only feigns injury on the course when he is playing badly not well. I told him she just could not be bothered to get her ball out of the bunker. Husband Tony arrives and confirms she is not very good at bunker play.

Pam is kept in the hospital and I am stranded there in golf gear and with no money or phone. I feel a little silly.

Chapter 19

The Next Appointment

It is months since I had the scan and at last I receive an appointment with Consultant David Porter. Sam goes with me and Mr Porter is in a good mood and so am I.

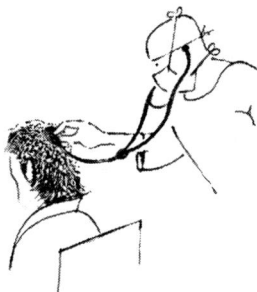

Sounds very strange in there

He tells me I should opt for the surgery now while I am young and fit and outlines the even worse consequences of not doing this; grapefruits were mentioned. Describing me as young and fit leaves me with doubts about his competency as below is a list of all the things wrong with my body—

Morton's Neuroma in left foot
Plantar fasciitus in right foot
Left knee fragile
Chest pain from old war wounds
Tendonitis in right arm

Despair
Brain tumour
Ear problems
Globus thing

They are digging the greens up at the golf club this winter to lay American Standard Greens which will be vastly superior but the prospect of temporary greens over the next few months does not appeal.

This is a better reason to have the surgery now, never mind the young and fit thing. The mind boggles with what I will be like afterwards. David Porter stops my mind boggling about what it will be like and it is not good news.

By the time I get home I am in a poor mood. I decide to call at the Doctor's surgery as I need my ears sorting out at least and not even The Long Ashton Surgery will be able to find anything else wrong with me. Even if they manage it things could not be any worse. I am now feeling nauseous. Alas they are installing new computers and are only dealing with emergencies so I don't bother.

My mood is a mess, my body is a mess and, as the golf season approaches its end, I have lots of matches to complete. I have little or no interest in them but unfortunately for them I have partners who are still keen and excited about it all.

The night has not been good and I am in a golf competition. I have lost interest and find it difficult to keep going. I am lucky in that I have a fun partner today and despite the rain we get round without any tragedies.

Anne is congratulated on completing a round with me without an ambulance having to be called.

I am playing at Bath in the County Scratch Knockout Final on Sunday with my young partner. We are playing Knowle.

This is the pair we knocked out in the semi-final last year on the fifth extra hole leaving them sulking and father telling off daughter for losing to a granny. He would probably have had apoplexy if he knew it was a granny with a heart bypass. The other 3 players are all off scratch or better and the ages of their mothers probably don't add up to my age. My tactics are to hit the ball anywhere and leave it to talented partner to sort out the result.

"Anyone see where that went?"

It is unbelievable.

We win!

I don't really know how.

I don't really know how we even got to the final.

One opponent is turning professional this week. I think I will start a new career as golf pro. Reality and a foul mood quickly set in as I realise that I will not be playing this well again if at all once David Porter has dug around in my brain. Long Ashton Ladies are fantastic and I get lots of messages of congratulation and ones of hope to cheer me up.

I now work myself up into a mood of profound despair and my itchy ears are giving me hell. I manage an appointment with GP and take Dr Grenfell apples from my trees in the hope that she will wave a magic branch as a panacea for all my ills. Alas she does not but I get some drops for my ears along with some sympathy.

I fancied being a doctor at one stage but my grades were not good enough to get into medical school. This is just as well because I would not be at all sympathetic and would just clear the surgery of all the moaners and groaners.

Miracles happen and I win the Long Ashton Open. I am now so mental anything can happen.

Chapter 20

Getting Going

I have given up on golf. The course is a mess and I cannot be bothered.

I decide to buy a new bike—an electric one. This will get me up and down Providence Lane and will get me around when I am banned from driving. Common sense says I will not be in any fit state to ride it then but my brain has little sense in it at the moment.

The Duracell Kid

I will sell my car to pay for it. They offer me peanuts for my car so I decide not to sell it. Tax and insurance run out on the car at the end of October so I complete a SORN, cancel my insurance and stick the car in the garage having sought advice on how to store it. Disconnect the battery, put WD40 on the alloy wheels and leave the handbrake off. Give it a good run before stuffing it in the garage.

A holiday is planned. We will all go cycling in Holland at half term. I spend ages filling in details on the Stena Line program and each time I reach the part where you pay, it will not take my money. Eventually I phone them and they know everything about what I have been trying to book and they take my money over the phone.

So off to Holland on our cycling holiday. We load up on the horse lorry to travel with cycles to Harwich. The horse lorry is ideal as it carries all five bikes and all five people. All goes well and everyone is excited as we cycle onto the ferry. We fasten up our bikes and find our cabins and off to sleep we go.

Next morning we disembark at some unearthly hour of the morning and look for a breakfast café. It is too early in the morning and everywhere is shut. We set off for the hotel with only one minor dead end and arrive about an hour later, find a café and have breakfast.

The following day we visit Delft. It is very picturesque and we enjoy a good lunch before we cycle back to the hotel.

Most of the places we go require considerable direction finding and information from maps and passers-by is constantly sought.

Next stop is La Hague for Sunday's day out.

It is Monday and we are off home. We have heard about hurricane St Jude and our sleep was disturbed all night by howling winds along the hotel corridor. We have to get to the ferry by 2.30pm and decide it would be wise to set off early as the wind may slow us down.

Off we go along the coastal cycle path unaware of how bad conditions are. We travelled into the worst of the wind, were blown off our cycles and had to walk a lot. St Jude is the saint for the hopeless and we were hopeless fools.

"I think my batteries have gone flat"

The wind blew the sand in our faces and we were well and truly sand blasted. Following this it rained just to soak us as well.

We made it! Heaven knows how. We were absolute idiots. We were exhausted and cold. Cycles are thrown down in a pile as we board the ferry.

Safely home and I have lost all my cards. I am lucky and a message on my phone tells me they are at the local police station. Joy of joys. Recovery of them is interesting as the police phones are not working and then the station is closed for the day. Good job I am not starving.

Chapter 21

Hospital Looms

I am learning to live life without a car and start cycling everywhere. The new bike is great. I cycle to Frenchay so see Consultant David Porter and receive a few instructions on what to do and a bit more information on how I will be afterwards.

If he knew the amount of time I have spent looking for my car in the golf club car park when it is not there because I have walked up, he might not have bothered to tell me I might have trouble with sequencing amongst other things.

I decide to take a different route back to Bristol and around 45 minutes later am back at Frenchay having gone round in a circle. Never mind, it is a nice day and I eventually make the city centre for some lunch. I go shopping to cheer myself up and soon have bought more stuff than will fit on the bike. I have to take the bus home, dump the shopping and get the bus back to collect my bike.

A brain operation can only improve things.

Nephew David is coming over from Australia in December together with boyfriend and boyfriend's mum. Brother Brian in Australia is not making expected progress with Guillen Barre Syndrome and is in hospital for tests. Christmas is coming and arrangements have to be made so I give David

Porter's secretary a ring to check that I will not have surgery before January. This is the 18 weeks and what I am expecting.

Oh dear, this was a mistake as a very cheerful woman tells me they have a date for me on the 12th November; she is very pleased but I am not. Only three weeks away and not what I was expecting. I nearly die on the spot. My calm laid back air has disappeared into the Ethernet or somewhere.

It all gets worse as she tells me David Porter will be taking me to a private hospital—The Spire—so a lot of stick will be coming my way. I may have to ditch my left wing views and vote for Nigel Farage—fat chance!

Well the BRI are very pleased at having obtained a Gamma knife which removes brain tumours without surgery. It is on the television and the world calls to tell me I now no longer need surgery. I look it up on the BRI web site and there it is with an email address for patients to make enquiries and so I do, not really expecting much to happen. I get a reassuring email back from Alison Cameron who is the consultant in charge. You just cannot believe how good these people are. My tumour in the anterior cranial fossa is not for the Gamma knife unless it recurs. So that is that. Still I got a nice encouraging email to reassure me that the right decision has been made. Not really surprising as David Porter appears to be pretty world class.

I now have a letter from The Spire and they want to see me on 4 November to stick pins in me and check I am alive before surgery. This messes up my bridge arrangements. The date and time of my surgery are also confirmed and I will have to get up at some unearthly time in the morning. I have been unaware that this hour actually existed ever since working stopped.

A long form to complete is enclosed, part of which asks about getting off to sleep. With all of this going on any sleep I get at all is a bonus.

Well I am now off to The Spire for the pre-surgery assessment. They have to be sure you are fit before you are wrecked. The lovely nurse comments that I only seem to go in for the big things—heart and brain; I confirm this as trivialities are not for me. Lots of bits of my body are swabbed as they don't want any nasty infections in the hospital, an ECG done and lots of fluids collected. I cycle home; it is dark and scary.

Well The Spire keeps altering the time for me to arrive. That is fine as I won't need to get up early although I doubt there will be much sleep somehow. I hope this lateness will leave me plenty of time to go clubbing after the brain surgery.

My last big social event at the golf club—

The Ladies AGM and Dinner.

It is wonderful, they are a great bunch of ladies and I have far too much to drink and then they are even more wonderful.

Chapter 22

The Time Has Arrived

On arrival at The Spire I am shown to my room by the concierge. I ask Sam if we should tip him or not but she knows no more than I do. Sam gets tea and biscuits but I am allowed nothing except for yet another backless front and some surgical stockings.

The concierge shows us the alarm button and says someone will come if it is pressed. He also shows us the alarm cord in the bathroom and says a cast of thousands will come if we pull that cord. When he has gone I have to stop Sam going to pull the cord just to see what happens. She is evil!

Consultant checks that I am actually here and have not done a runner. I tell my surgeon that although I am not a brain surgeon death would be preferable to waking up like the Hartlepool lot that hung a monkey.

The anaesthetist calls. I try to swap places with Sam but it does not work. The anaesthetist says I seem very relaxed but he obviously knows little about swans or ducks and their swimming techniques.

I now have to don the backless front and surgical stockings. Well things run a little late but eventually I am carted off to the operating theatre.

I just hope I have a working brain left afterwards.

"Tell the anaesthetist I'm still wide awake"

The anaesthetist does get me out for the count. As with my heart operation I know not what happens next.

I certainly know what happened post-surgery. I am surrounded by brain surgeon, anaesthetist and lots of nurses and am in pain like I have never known before. The medical team start asking me questions such as "Do I know where I am?" Of course I know but I don't much care because of the pain. Poor David Porter gets abuse but he told me there was not a lot of pain with this surgery. The team decide my brain is OK and start injecting the morphine very quickly thereby preventing a further torrent of abusive language.

The next thing I know is waking up in intensive care the following morning feeling very strange.

A lovely young male nurse comes along, washes me, changes the sheets and I think I had breakfast. The same happened the next day but a female nurse accompanied the young male and I swear I did nothing wrong the first day as to need a chaperone.

I have a scan to make sure they have left some brain and soon end up out of intensive care and into my own room. Surgeon and anaesthetist check daily to ensure all is well. Nurses are excellent too and Emma brings them a cake she made herself using fresh eggs from my hens. The only snag is being woken up every two hours during the night for tests and this took a bit of time to get over on arrival home.

I point out to George and Emma that the bag over the bed puts fluid into my body while the bag under the bed collects fluid from my body. When they are empty and full, they just swap them over. Emma and George are a little sceptical about this. They all decline to see the bag under the bed on the other side which is collecting bits of my brain. Sam tells me not to expect a change of sheets, a wash and breakfast in bed when I am at the Mantzos Mansion. George offers but his price is a little high.

My head is completely enclosed by a large turban like bandage presumably to keep my cranium on. One day the nurse tells me that they will take it off tomorrow. I protest and tell him that my head will subsequently fall apart. He smiles and assures me it will not and the next day the whole turban is unwrapped.

I am very worried about this but in the morning I find my skull still intact. I am happy.

I am not happy as the nurse tells me the staples have to come out next. Sam offers to do this with her staple remover. I tell her in no uncertain terms that she is not going anywhere near my head. A nurse arrives to take out the staples, which is not a pleasant experience. I am now allowed to leave the hospital, along with medication and instructions about what and what not to do. I cannot remember many of these instructions so in the end just do whatever. Leaving hospital is the same as last time. Although the outside world seems very strange it has not really altered since I last saw it.

Chapter 23

End

Well I am tired, sleep a lot and have headaches and am dead to the world by 9.00pm. I am well looked after at the Mantzos Mansion and soon go home.

I walk to the golf club alone as it is ladies' day and am greeted with joy and amazement at my survival and how well I look. So many offers of help and support come my way. You just cannot believe how good people are.

I am now out walking and doing a bit of work in the garden, headaches are subsiding and painkillers rarely needed though my head is fuzzy and sore. Next step is shopping in Bristol.

I have now realised that my sense of smell has gone as warned. Wounds are slowly healing; scars from surgery are virtually invisible or well hidden. David Porter is a genius. Not yet fit enough to swing a golf club even though I can now make it through a day till 10.00pm or later.

Instructions on anticonvulsant tablets say to take them for a month and to see my GP when the 28 tablets run out. GP says 28 days counts as a month which is worrying as it isn't February. This means I am now very anxious about events to follow but GP says just to go to hospital if anything goes wrong.

Ho bloody ho!

I guess Christmas is only a couple of weeks away.

Scalp feels very tight with lots of itching and tingling. Apparently this is a sign nerve endings are healing. Headaches are subsiding and are more intermittent.

So far so good. Nothing much has gone wrong. I have bought oil scented with lavender to aid sleeping knowing full well before I bought it I could not smell. Surgery has certainly not improved my brain. My first session at the bridge club confirms this as I finish in the bottom half of the field.

It is now time for the bike to emerge as the bus timetables are not all that reliable. I tentatively set off in the new yellow luminous Christmas present jacket and am terrified. However, confidence grows and I make it back from shopping safely. Another little hurdle crossed.

The weather is getting warmer so golf beckons. First session in the golf range does not go too well. Shots are a little haphazard to say the least and a headache follows. Things do however rapidly improve.

My rewired brain should
see me winning
everything at golf and I
will soon shoot up the
bridge league tables.

Not lost any of the old magic

The chickens are returning home after their winter holidays and will find a change in their habitat as I am not having them scratching up my lawn again.

**As both my brain and heart are now fixed
and with two lots of major surgery survived,
I can now consider myself immortal again.
Nothing else can possibly go wrong.**

**As additional insurance I intend never to go
near my GP again so nothing else can be found
to be faulty with my body. This is especially
true if I have any further ear issues.**

**Alas I find out that for the rest of my life I
must avoid the sports of rugby and boxing.**

The itchy ear remains.

**Sunderland have beaten Manchester
United in the semi-final of the cup and
so I am off to Wembley. Hooray!**

Lightning Source UK Ltd.
Milton Keynes UK
UKOW02f0753130815

256862UK00001B/29/P

9 781491 896662